MONEY MONEY MONEY

by RUTH BELOV GROSS

Pictures by LESLIE JACOBS

SCHOLASTIC BOOK SERVICES

NEW YORK · TORONTO · LONDON · AUCKLAND · SYDNEY

ISBN 0-590-09189-1

13 12 11 10 9 8 7 6 5 4 3 2   1 2 3/8
Printed in U.S.A.   02

For my mother
and for Evie

A long time ago there was no money at all
in the world. People didn't need money.
They got everything they needed by trading things.

The people who lived in Egypt many
thousands of years ago traded things.
They traded some of the things they didn't need
for other things they did need.

The people who lived in Greece many
thousands of years ago traded things too.

Will you give me that
jar of honey if I give you
some figs?

Yes, I'll trade with you.
Take the honey — but
give me <u>all</u> your figs.

All over the world,
people traded with each other.

There is a special name for this kind of trading.
The name is *barter*.

Most of the time, barter was a good way
of getting things. There was one trouble with
barter, though. What happened when you had
something to trade but nobody wanted it?

We don't want any sandals.
But if you have some bananas,
we'll trade with you.

I have just made a
fine pair of sandals.
Will you give me some
arrowheads for these sandals?

I don't have any bananas.

Sorry.

If nobody wanted the things you had,
you were out of luck! But —

—what if you had something that almost everybody wanted? Then it was easy to make a trade.

In some places, a long time ago, you could
always make a trade if you had a cow.

If I give you this
nice fat cow, will you
give me those knives?

I don't need a cow.
But I'll take it anyhow and
give you the knives.

Hmmm. I wonder why
he'll take my cow. He said
he doesn't need a cow...

The people around here
are always looking for
nice fat cows. I'm sure
I can trade this cow
for something I want...

Here is the cow.

Here are the knives.

In other places, a long time ago, you could always make a trade if you had pigs or goats or sheep. In all these places, the people used their animals the way we use money.

So you can say that cows and pigs and goats and sheep were an early kind of money.

Animals weren't the only things people
used for money, a long time ago.

In some places, people used salt for money.
Everybody wanted salt for their food.
In Rome, the soldiers were even paid
in salt!

In some places, people used corn and grain
for money.

In some places, people used little shells
for money. They were called cowrie
shells. You could put them on a string
and wear them around your neck.
They were supposed to be lucky.

In some places, people used spades and
shovels and knives for money. People
needed these tools for their crops
and animals.

But there was one trouble with the things
people used for money.

What if the cows or pigs or goats or sheep
got sick?
What if the salt got wet — and washed away?
What if the corn or grain got spoiled?
What if the cowrie shells got smashed?
What if the tools got broken?

Then what could people use for money?

My money doesn't feel well.

After a while, people found better things
to use for money. They began to use
pieces of metal —

copper and

bronze and

iron and

gold and

silver.

A piece of metal wouldn't get sick.
A piece of metal wouldn't wash away in
the rain.
A piece of metal wouldn't get spoiled.
A piece of metal wouldn't get smashed.
A piece of metal wouldn't get broken.
And you could carry your metal money
around with you.

You could make pots and tools and other
useful things out of metal. You could make
beautiful necklaces and rings and bracelets too.

When people began to use metal for money,
they used all sizes and shapes of metal.
They used lumps of metal, and chunks of metal,
and bars of metal.

How much could you buy if you had a chunk
of copper? The heavier your chunk of copper was,
the more you could buy with it.

But how did you know how heavy it was?
You had to weigh it.

When somebody gave you a piece of metal,
you weighed it. When you gave somebody else
a piece of metal, *he* weighed it. That way,
nobody cheated anybody. The metal was weighed
every time a person gave another person some

copper or
bronze or
iron or
gold or
silver.

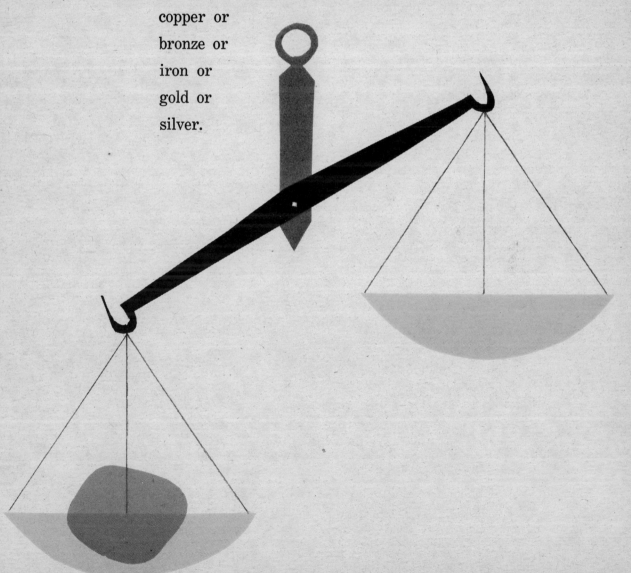

Weighing the metal was a lot of trouble
for everybody.

Just think what it would be like if the
man in the grocery store had to weigh your money
every time he sold you some cookies!

At last some men had a good idea. This is
what they decided to do: A man would weigh
a piece of metal once. He would put a mark on it
to show how much it weighed. After that,
the metal would not have to be weighed again.

The piece of metal was now a *coin*. Everybody
could look at it and see how much it was worth.

One day, almost three thousand years ago,
the king of a country called Lydia
made a new law.

The king said that the people of Lydia
were not allowed to weigh their own metal
and mark it any more. The king's men were
the only ones who had the right
to make metal into coins.

The king's money was the first real money
people had. We say it was the first real
money because it was made by the government,
just like our money is today.

In Lydia it was against the law to make
your own money. Any man who tried
would get into trouble.

The king of Lydia
made his coins out of
gold and silver. The coins
looked like lumpy buttons.

Soon the governments of other countries
were making coins too.

Coins made in Greece
a long time ago looked
something like our pennies
and nickels and dimes,
only they were thicker
and not quite round.

Some of the coins made in
Rome did not look like our
coins at all. This coin
was bigger than a slice of
bread. It weighed more than
a pound.

Before long, many more countries had their
own metal coins.

Let's stop now to see what we know about money.
This is what we know:

In the very beginning, before there was any money
at all, people just traded with each other.

Later on, animals were money. Salt was money.
Corn and grain and shells and tools
were money too.

After a while, pieces of metal were money.
And then people began to make their pieces of
metal into coins.

The first real money was made by the government
of a country called Lydia.
Other governments made money for their people
after that. People feel safer when the government
is in charge of making the money they use.

These things did not happen in a day.
They took a long time to happen.
And they happened at different times in
different places.

People in some parts of the world were
still using cows for money when people in other
parts of the world were using metal coins.

About three hundred and fifty years ago,
some people from England came to live in America.
They came to settle in colonies.

When they lived in England, they used
metal coins. But when they came to settle
in America they did not bring many coins
with them. And the king of England wouldn't
let anyone make coins in the American colonies.

So the settlers didn't have much money.
But they found ways to get the things they needed.

What do you think they did?

They traded with each other.

If you will make
shoes for my horse,
I will make you a
new wig.

Good. I need
a new wig.

They used corn for money, and they used
cows for money. They used beaver skins for
money, and they used tobacco for money.
They used fish and peas and wheat for
money, and they used nails and bullets for money.

They even used these things to pay their
bills and to pay their taxes.

People almost always tried to pay their
taxes with the skinniest cows they had.

I've come to pay my taxes.
Here's my cow.

Do you call that
a cow?

TAX
COLLECTOR

In many of the American colonies the settlers
used little beads made from shells.
The shell beads were called *wampum*. Wampum
was what the Indians used for money.

Six white beads were worth about a penny.
Black beads were worth twice as much as white beads.

If you had wampum, you could buy beaver skins
from the Indians. You could also buy
things from other settlers.

The Indians made wampum out of clam shells and
periwinkle shells. They strung the wampum beads
on thin strips of deer hide. The Indians made
beautiful belts and bracelets out of wampum too.

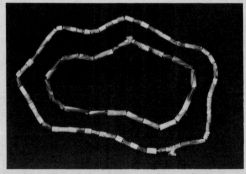

THE CHASE MANHATTAN BANK MONEY MUSEUM

The settlers used French coins and Dutch coins
and English coins and Spanish coins.

They got some of the coins by selling fish and
flour and lumber and furs to other countries.

And they got some of the coins from pirates.
The pirates came to buy food for themselves
and tar and pitch and turpentine for their ships.
They paid the settlers with the gold and silver
coins they took from other ships at sea.

Again and again the settlers asked the
king of England to let them make their own money.
Every time they asked, the king said no.
He said it was against the law for the
settlers in the colonies to make their own money.

The settlers did not like the king's law
about money. They did not like some other laws
the king made for them. They decided they
did not want the king of England to make any of
their laws. They wanted to make their own laws.

So the colonies had a war with England.
It was called the American Revolution.
The colonies won the war.

That was about two hundred years ago.

After the American Revolution, the colonies
did not belong to England any more.
They were not colonies now. They were *states*.
They were the United States of America.
Now they could make their own laws.

Soon the people in the United States had
their own coins. The coins were made by the
new government.

This is what two of the coins looked like:

An eagle — $10

This coin was made of gold.

A half cent

A half cent was made of copper.

The United States government made the coins,
but for a long time it let the banks make
the paper money.

Now the government makes all of our money —
all of our coins and all of our paper money.
If anybody else tries to make coins or
paper money, he gets into trouble!

The United States was not the first country to use
paper money. People in China used paper money
long before any settlers came to America.
China was ruled by an emperor, and only the
emperor's men could make the paper money.
If anybody else tried to make paper money,
he was in trouble.

Money. Money. Money. It comes in very handy.

Children use money to buy ice cream cones.
They use it to buy birthday presents for their
friends. Sometimes they use it to buy lunch at school.

Grownups use coins and paper money too.
But they also use *checks*.

And they use *credit cards*.

Checks and credit cards are things that people
can use instead of the money the government makes.

A check is like a little letter to the bank.
It tells the bank to give some of your money
to someone.
But you can only use a check if you have
money in the bank!

A credit card is something people use
when they want to pay later. Many people
use a credit card to buy gas for their cars.
Then they don't have to pay for the gas right away.

Some people think they are getting things free
when they use a credit card. That isn't true
at all. Even with a credit card, you have to pay
for the things you buy! And sometimes you
have to pay extra.

Now we know some of the things we use for money today.

We use money for money.
We use checks.
We use credit cards.

But even today some people still use barter —
especially children.

Some of the strange things people have used for money

Things to eat

Tea was money in China. You could buy a horse or a camel if you had enough tea.

Cocoa beans were money in Mexico. The Aztec Indians used sacks of cocoa beans to buy the things they wanted.

Coconuts were money for people who lived on some islands near India.

Things to use

Fish hooks were money for Aleut Indians of Alaska.

Blankets were money for Indian tribes in Canada.

Arrows were money in many places.

Things to wear and to show

A string of shells was money for Indians
in America and for people on islands in the
Pacific Ocean.

Whales' teeth were money on the island of
Fiji. You could buy a canoe with one tooth.

Hair from an elephant's tail was money
in Africa. A bracelet made out of elephant hair
was supposed to be lucky.

Feathers were money on some islands in
the Pacific Ocean.

The biggest and heaviest money in the world
was a round stone with a hole in the middle.
It was called a **Yap stone.** Yap stones were money
on the Caroline Islands in the Pacific Ocean.
Some Yap stones were twelve feet high—as big as
two tall men. If you had a small Yap stone,
you could buy a pig or a thousand coconuts.

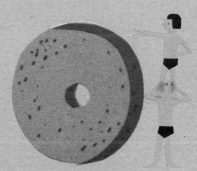